I'm Fine

Paul Mendez

BookLeaf
Publishing

India | USA | UK

Presentation by *BookLeaf Publishing*

Web: www.bookleafpub.com

E-mail: info@bookleafpub.com

ISBN: 978-93-5744-344-9

First edition 2022

DEDICATION

To Emily, Giovanna, and the lone butterfly that has quietly followed me

I'm fine

It started as a placeholder
A phrase to chase away feelings 'til I was bolder.
It was a way to avoid deeper prodding,
A manifestation towards a destiny I wanted.

I said "I'm fine" to those who asked
All the while worrying about my own past.
I also thought about their state of mind
Asking: "what other response is there to find."

In each case, with every personal turmoil
I reminded myself this was my burden with
which to toil.

I am fine

It's all under control, I've learned to manage.
There are those worse and those better that
      cannot cope.
Still, I'm a dope for comparing my ills to an
      other's
Yet I stay my response because this problem is
      my own.

There was never a moment where I was so low,
      it was never an option.
I was never taught to allow myself to wallow.
My only response has been to find a solution, to
      avoid the negative;
A perspective that never strayed from the
      underlying thought that I am fine.

Unfortunately, with time, you come to learn
      more about yourself
Which brings greater realization that you might
      have actually been led astray.

I'm fine*

The question that leads to this response is not a
  daily occurrence.
Even if it were, each response is different;
I don't know how I feel until I utter these same
  words.
There's an appendix to be filled about each
  instance of this interaction.

There is an infinite variability of affective reason
Which grows and changes alongside life itself.
People, as islands, develop traits uniquely.
But dialogue is much more difficult than
  monologue.

Information has become a manner of
  self-preservation
But definitions also change, creating new
  expectations of private and public discourse.

Defined

Not good, not bad. Not okay, or great, or could
        be better.
Any other response would carry weight in some
        direction.
But "Fine" is dismissive. It stops.
It creates a point of finality.

It reflects a small part of a larger whole;
A simple piece that rarely begs context
It does not need coaxing
For it is rarely alone.

But its definition is almost irrelevant.
It is the context that determines its nature.

I'm "fine"

Every perspective affixes its own meaning.
Fine for one is not the same for an other.
It covers meaning across a fuller spectrum
And yet it is continually used to portray the
       center.

To use this phrase is to trust the other to choose
       the appropriate definition:
A request that rarely receives the expected
       response.
The missing element is true mutual
       understanding;
Some identities are rarely seen beyond the self.

There is mutual dependency; active involvement
       from all parties.
The challenge comes from equal interest and
       investment.

(I'm fine)

Good and bad are part of a spectrum.
You cannot have either extreme consistently,
      through life.
They are both parts of each other
Like mouth and rectum.

We are taught to seek happiness but not its
      counterpart;
Taught to avoid the negative rather than embrace it
      as a part of ourselves, as a part of its other.
We have yet learned to appreciate our neutrality
      and its role as the norm.
We call it boredom, complacency – as an affront –
      when it means development and peace.

I am fine because that should be my natural state.
It is the world around me that makes me not so.

#imfine

Social presence is no longer purely physical
The masks we wear cross various lines and must
        satiate the norm.
Cries for help are both easier to share and
        ignore,
Coming from instances that have not been
        previously defined.

The "I" looks upon other media to find relief
Yet the media is still learning to look back.
The calls are too loud but often without aim
They are a silent scream for attention, lost
        among a forest.

A simple response is rarely enough.
There are deep roots, demanding time that does
        not yet exist.

I'm Fine.

There is confidence and authority in the words we
        speak.
Though we may feel timid and apprehensive
We can tell others those feelings are untrue.
Tone is often louder than the words spoken.

I imply that I don't want to continue repeating this
        phrase
Thoughts left unspoken are not easily translated.
Still, there is some understanding,
The subconscious inherits a new awkwardness to
        avoid.

Distance is not solely attributed to the physical.
Emotions can be disconnected, the dialogue wants
        for something that no longer exists.

They don't think I'm fine

There is a double-edge.
There is often no need to pursue this line of
      thought.
I provide solace, an answer sought
But people are complex.

Relationships are a dialogue:
They depend on interaction and the wariness of
      multiple parties.
While I provide enough to find another topic,
There are thoughts that continue, considering
      that the answer given is not apt.

But dialogue is not impervious to change.
Though, a person is obtusely simple: forgetting
      they are a part of people.

I'm. Fine.

Emphasis and inflection can often do more than
     any communicable words.
Sometimes it creates irreparable damage and a
     shift in understanding.
People receive others as fixed properties
When we should recognize each other as
     malleable and dynamic.

Singular emotions can lead to simple
     misinterpretation and long-term effects
Because people are often rigid when viewed on
     smaller scales of time.
Because a dialogue considers the many over the
     one
It is not just my implication but the imprint left
     upon others.

I'm bored of this response, yet it is a constant;
Requiring emotional exposition internally and
     communicated clearly.

I'm ---

It is not always easy to say.
Behind the response there are young thoughts
       and emotions unexplored.
It becomes difficult to choose between inclusion
       and omission.
I worry they may choose differently and ask for
       more.

I stop myself, I slow down.
I allow thoughts to process and consider the
       opportunity presented.
I want to say more, I want them to listen
But I keep my feelings, I say nothing new.

I know I'm not lying.
I know nothing is wrong.

I'm fine..

Consider the other.
I can't seem to not.
They don't always want to talk about my
        problems;
I barely do.

I'm left with my own thoughts
I have to figure it out: my self.
Then again, our definition of a problem is not
        the same
Problems are hardly significant and almost
        purely happenstance.

After all, it is only the individual we have to
        look after.
Community is just another part of the whole.

I'm Fine…

I want a response.
I want a follow-up question.
I want to say more.
I want interactive dialogue.

Why won't I respond with anything else?
Why won't they ask?
Why don't I volunteer more information?
Why don't I force the dialogue?

There is an endless casting of blame.
There is no definitive acceptance of such.

fe'nimi

The phrase continues to hold its place.
It does so though I am not active.
I can communicate my feelings to others
Though I don't quite understand them myself.

I am irresponsible to keep them to myself
More so that I allow them to harm others.
They are more than my own
I cannot brush these feelings away.

Repetition allows a word to lose its meaning.
Repetition also allows meaning to be found
       again.

imfine

I speak under my breath
Barely mumbling over my shame.
I worry that my thoughts have no reason, that
they are not justified.
I hope they won't hear.

I have little interest in this interaction, or
anything
The day is a blur of routine.
I am not an active participant
I don't want anyone to notice and revive a
Romantic self.

I don't tell anyone.
I am absolutely not fine.

I'M FINE

Finally, I lash out.
Obviously there is some festering problem.
Though I scream as though I want them to stop
      asking
I lie to myself and everyone around me.

There is no time to think about the consequences
      of my actions.
I barely have the capacity.
I can't even speak against myself
I am embarrassed to have intimidated those
      closest to me.

There is no regret in acting differently than
      others may expect.
Still, something is wrong.

I'm not fine

I may not always need to be honest to those
       around me
But I do need to be honest with myself.
I need to recognize the lapses in my life
I need to recognize those events that cause my
       strife.

I may not be fine but I have an end for which to
       strive
It teaches me to look in covered places.
I struggle with keeping distance with those
       around me
But that distance is not held within.

I am truthful about my thoughts and responses
I also learn in linear time which is its own
       hindrance.

Am I fine?

I can't bring myself to approach others with
      these thoughts
I can – and must – address my actions.
It is not the responsibility of anyone else
I must find contentment with the events
      encompassing my life.

This requires confronting the uncomfortable
I must figure out as much about myself as well
      as those around me.
There is a root that remains underground
It may not need separation but it merits
      discovery.

We often find the simplest questions become the
      most perplexing
I often find there is more I have yet to uncover.

I'm fine?

These are not new feelings
Rather simply: a new understanding.
Thoughts and emotions I've felt before,
Given a new perspective

It helps to think positively
Something I need to practice.
I say I'm fine
Uncertain in the truth it carries..

This is helpful; a better way of living.
Right?

I am fine.

I have not learned everything about myself
For I have not finished living.
Though I understand my range:
The feelings I have and that to which they react.

But I am fine.
I speak without subtext or hesitation.
Though I still may not be, I know that I am not
Which is more than I understood before.

Manifestation is not a simple spell
It is not enough to be said, I must also mean.

I'm fine.

There is a different context now
I am a different person.
Though people still know me
They don't know me as I am now.

They know who I was.
My response does not change
But its meaning does.
There is no puzzle to solve.

What started as a volatile neutral has become a
       true center.
There is no additional context needed, for this
       simple phrase is used appropriately.

9 789357 443449